W9-AOX-783

The Life and Work of...

Wassily Kandinsky

Paul Flux

Heinemann Library
Chicago, Illinois

Designed by Celia Floyd
Illustrations by Sam Thompson
Originated by Ambassador Litho Ltd.
Printed and bound in China

06
10 9 8 7 6 5 4 3 2

Library of Congress Cataloging-in-Publication Data
Flux, Paul, 1952-
  Wassily Kandinsky / Paul Flux.
      p. cm. -- (The life and work of...)
Includes bibliographical references and index.
Summary: Presents a brief overview of the life and work of this Russian artist, describing and giving examples of his work.
  ISBN 1-58810-607-1 (lib. bdg.)   ISBN 1-4034-0006-7 (pbk. bdg.)
  1. Kandinsky, Wassily, 1866-1944--Juvenile literature. 2.
Artists--Russia (Federation)--Biography--Juvenile literature. [1.
Kandinsky, Wassily, 1866-1944. 2. Artists. 3. Painting, Russian.] I.
Title. II. Series.
  N6999.K33 F58 2002
  759.7--dc21
                        2001003969

KANDINSKY, W
c. 1

Acknowledgments
The author and publishers are grateful to the following for permission to reproduce copyright material:
p. 4, Bridgeman Art Library; pp. 5, 22, RMN; p. 7, Tretyakov Gallery, Moscow; p. 9, © Foto/Städtische Galerie im Lenbachhaus; pp. 10, 16, Hulton Archive; p. 11, Buhrle Collection, Zurich; p. 13, Private Collection; p. 15, Kunstammlung Nordrhein-Westfalen, Dusseldorf; p. 17, Solomon R. Guggenheim Museum, New York; p. 19, Musée National d'Art Moderne, Paris; p. 20, AKG; p. 21, Lenbachlaus, Munich; pp. 23, 25, 27, 29, David Heald/The Solomon R. Guggenheim Foundation, New York; p. 26, Roger Viollet.

Cover photograph (*Yellow, Red, Blue,* Wassily Kandinsky) reproduced with permission of Bridgman Art Library/Musée National d'Art Moderne, Paris.

Special thanks to Katie Miller for her comments in the preparation of this book.

Every effort has been made to contact copyright holders of any material reproduced in this book. Any omissions will be rectified in subsequent printings if notice is given to the publisher.

Some words are shown in bold, **like this.** You can find out what they mean by looking in the glossary.

Contents

Who Was Wassily Kandinsky?

Wassily Kandinsky was a Russian painter. He is well known for his **abstract** pictures of colorful shapes. He was also a teacher who **inspired** many other artists with his ideas.

4

Wassily was one of the first artists to paint abstract shapes in bright colors. His paintings do not always look like something from real life. His pictures show new ways of putting colored shapes together.

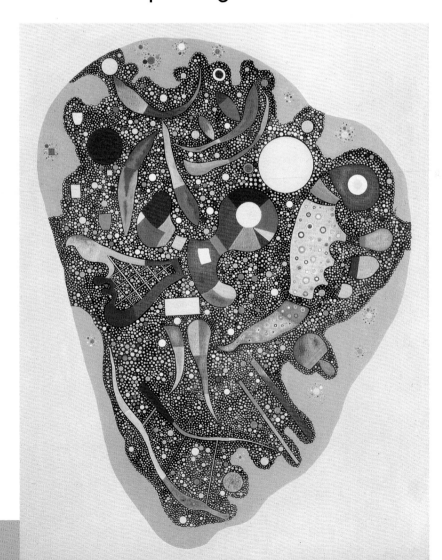

Colorful Ensemble, 1938

Early Years

Wassily Kandinsky was born on December 4, 1866, in **Moscow,** Russia. In 1871, his parents got a **divorce.** Wassily moved to Odessa, Russia, to live with his aunt.

In 1889, Wassily visited northern Russia. There he saw art made by the local people. He loved what he saw. He began to paint pictures of the places he knew.

The Port of Odessa, 1890

Teaching and Learning

In 1892, Wassily married his distant cousin Anya Shemiakina. A year later he began to teach **law** classes at the University of **Moscow.** By 1896, Wassily knew he wanted to be an artist.

In 1900, Wassily began to study art in Munich, Germany. There he helped start a group of artists called the Phalanx. Wassily made this poster to tell people about their first **exhibition.**

Poster for the first Phalanx exhibition, 1901

Experiments with Color

In 1905, Wassily saw an **exhibition**. The painters there used strong colors. Henri Matisse was the leader of the group. After seeing the exhibition, Wassily took more risks with his use of color.

The Blue Rider, 1903

The rider in this painting is Saint George, the **patron saint** of England. He is riding away to make the world a better place to live. Wassily wanted his paintings to change the world.

A Fresh Start

Wassily traveled a lot in France and Russia. In 1908, he moved back to Munich, Germany. The paintings that he did there were more colorful and less **realistic** than ones he had done before.

Wassily painted this picture in Murnau, a small town in Germany. He has not tried to show us exactly what he saw there. The painting is more of an **impression** of the view.

Road at Murnau, 1909

New Ideas

In 1911, Wassily helped plan the first **"Blue Rider" exhibition.** All the artists in the Blue Riders group were trying to find new ways to paint. Wassily was also **experimenting** with writing poetry.

14

Composition IV, 1911

Between 1910 and 1939, Wassily painted ten large pictures he called "Compositions." This was one of the first **abstract** pictures ever painted. It is made of shapes and blocks of color, rather than real objects.

Painting Shapes

Wassily and Anya got **divorced** in 1911. By 1913, Wassily had decided to paint only **abstract** shapes. His paintings were shown in New York, which is shown here. People had to look carefully at Wassily's paintings to understand them.

Small Pleasures, 1913

Wassily now tried to fill his pictures with shapes and colors. He said that this painting made him think of the sound of small, falling, drops of water.

Back to Moscow

After **World War I** began in 1914, Wassily returned to **Moscow**. There he met Nina Andreevskaya. They got married in 1917.

When the war ended, Wassily hoped that his homeland would be a good place to live. His paintings were bright and hopeful.

In Gray, 1919

Teaching Art

In December 1921, Wassily and Nina left **Moscow** to travel to Germany. Wassily began teaching at the **Bauhaus,** a famous art school. He was very excited about this.

This is one of the last paintings that Wassily did before moving from Russia to Germany. He was still painting colored shapes. He thought that a circle was the perfect shape.

Red Spot II, 1921

At the Bauhaus

Wassily was very busy with his teaching at the **Bauhaus,** but he still painted often. Other artists at the school designed furniture. One of them named this chair after Kandinsky.

This is one of Wassily's most important paintings from this time. The colors, shapes, and spaces between shapes all balance out. The other artists Wassily worked with at the Bauhaus **inspired** some of his best work.

Composition VIII, 1923

The End of the Bauhaus

In 1933, **Adolf Hitler** took power in Germany. He did not like the kind of art the **Bauhaus** was teaching. The Bauhaus was closed, and most of the teachers left the country.

This is one of the last paintings that Wassily did in Germany. He knew he would not be safe there any longer. In December 1933, he left for Paris, France.

Decisive Pink, 1932

Living in Paris

In Paris, Wassily tried to make money by selling his paintings. These were difficult years for him. Having an **exhibition** in 1937 helped more people see his work.

In 1939, **World War II** began. In 1940, German soldiers entered Paris, but Wassily stayed in the city. He still painted many well-known shapes, like the red circle here. What kinds of feelings does this painting suggest to you?

Around the Circle, 1940

Final Days

Wassily became ill during the war. He still wanted to find new ways to show his thoughts in his art. He used bright colors and shapes to show what he was feeling.

Twilight, 1943

Wassily died on December 13, 1944. This is one of the last paintings he did. He is remembered best for his work on new ways of painting.

Timeline

1866	Wassily Kandinsky is born in **Moscow,** Russia on December 4.
1871	Wassily's parents **divorce**. Wassily is brought up by an aunt.
1886	Wassily studies **law** at Moscow University.
1892	He marries his cousin, Anya Shemiakina.
1893	Wassily teaches law classes at Moscow University.
1896	He begins to study art seriously and moves to Munich, Germany.
1900	Wassily studies at the Munich Academy of Art.
1901	Wassily helps to start the Phalanx group.
1911	Wassily and his wife get divorced. He helps organize the first **"Blue Rider" exhibition.**
1914	**World War I** begins.
1917	Wassily marries Nina Andreevskaya. They have a son, Vsevdod.
1920	Vsevdod dies.
1921	Wassily and Nina return to Germany.
1922	Wassily starts work at the **Bauhaus** art school.
1923	Wassily has one-man show in New York.
1933	The Bauhaus is closed. Wassily moves to Paris, France.
1944	On December 13, Wassily dies at the age of 78.

Glossary

abstract   kind of art that does not try to show people or things. It uses shape and color to make the picture.

Adolf Hitler   German leader from 1933 to 1945

Bauhaus   famous art school in Germany

Blue Rider   group of artists in Germany, started in 1911, led by Wassily and Franz Marc

divorce   to end a marriage

exhibition   public display of works of art

experiment   to try new things

impression   sense of what is there

inspired   when someone gives good ideas to someone else

law   rules of a country

Moscow   capital city of Russia

patron saint   holy person who watches over a country

realistic   trying to show something as it really is

World War I   war in Europe that lasted from 1914 to 1918

World War II   war fought in Europe, Africa, and Asia from 1939 to 1945

Index

More Books to Read

Flux, Paul. *Color.* Chicago: Heinemann Library, 2001.

Flux, Paul. *Shape.* Chicago: Heinemann Library, 2001.

Kutschbach, Doris. *The Blue Rider: The Yellow Cow Sees the World in Blue.* New York: Prestel Publishing, 1997.

More Artwork to See

Blue Mountain. 1908–09. Guggenheim Museum, New York, N.Y.

Improvisation 30 (Cannons). 1913. The Art Institute of Chicago, Illinois.

Orange. 1923. The Fine Art Museum of San Francisco, California.